D1195884

● Smithsonian

Exploring the
the

New Hampshire
Colony

by Elizabeth Raum

CAPSTONE PRESS
a capstone imprint

Smithsonian books are published by Capstone Press,
1710 Roe Crest Drive, North Mankato, Minnesota 56003
www.capstonepub.com

Library of Congress Cataloging-in-Publication Data
Names: Raum, Elizabeth, author.
Title: Exploring the New Hampshire Colony / by Elizabeth Raum.
Description: North Mankato, Minnesota: Capstone Press, [2017] | Series:
    Smithsonian. Exploring the 13 Colonies | Includes bibliographical
    references and index. | Audience: Grades 4–6.
Identifiers: LCCN 2016002545 | ISBN 9781515722366 (library binding) | ISBN
    9781515722496 (paperback) | ISBN 9781515722625 (ebook (PDF))
Subjects: LCSH: New Hampshire—History—Colonial period, ca.
    1600–1775—Juvenile literature.
    | New Hampshire—History—1775–1865—Juvenile literature.
Classification: LCC F37 .R38 2017 | DDC 974.2/02—dc23
LC record available at http://lccn.loc.gov/2016002545

Editorial Credits
Gina Kammer, editor; Richard Parker, designer; Eric Gohl, media researcher;
Kathy McColley, production specialist

Our very special thanks to Stephen Binns at the Smithsonian Center for Learning and Digital Access for
his curatorial review. Capstone would also like to thank Kealy Gordon, Smithsonian Institution Product
Development Manager, and the following at Smithsonian Enterprises: Christopher A. Liedel, President;
Carol LeBlanc, Senior Vice President; Brigid Ferraro, Vice President; Ellen Nanney, Licensing Manager.

Photo Credits
Alamy: Everett Collection Historical, 41; Capstone: 4; Corbis: Photo Images/Lee Snider, 31; Courtesy
of Army Art Collection, U.S. Army Center of Military History: 38; Dreamstime: Julia Freeman-
Woolpert, 11; Getty Images: Culture Club, 9, Hulton Archive, 36, Stringer/Fotosearch, 35, Stringer/
MPI, 21, Stringer/Three Lions, 14; Granger, NYC: 16, 28, 30, 32, 34; The Image Works Archives: 17,
24; Newscom: Danita Delimont Photography/DanitaDelimont.com/Angel Wynn, 10; North Wind
Picture Archives: cover, 6, 7, 8, 12, 13, 18, 19, 20, 22, 23, 25, 26, 29 (bottom), 33, 37, 39 (all); Shutterstock:
Atlaspix, 40; Wikimedia: Craig Michaud, 29 (top), Public Domain, 27

Design Elements: Shutterstock

Printed and bound in the USA.
009669F16

Table of Contents

Introduction:
The 13 Colonies

New Hampshire was one of the 13 original American Colonies. A **colony** is a territory under the control of a distant country. In the case of the 13 Colonies, the distant country was England. England looked to New Hampshire and its other colonies as a source of wealth and power. For example, New Hampshire could provide valuable **natural resources** like fish and lumber to European markets. Each of the 13 Colonies was unique in what it offered England.

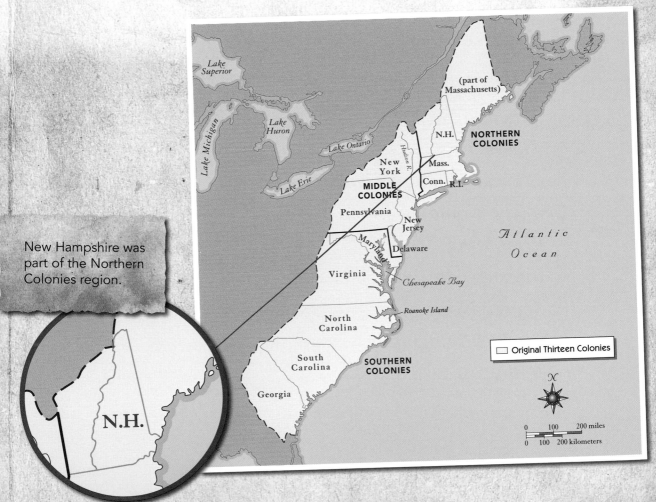

New Hampshire was part of the Northern Colonies region.

colony—a place that is settled by people from another country and is controlled by that country

The Original 13 Colonies

The first permanent European settlement in each colony:

Virginia	1607	Delaware	1638
Massachusetts	1620	Pennsylvania	1643
		North Carolina	1653
New York	1624	New Jersey	1660
Connecticut	1633	South Carolina	1670
Maryland	1634	Georgia	1733
Rhode Island	1636		

How the Colonies Began

Colonies began in different ways too. Virginia, for example, was established in 1607 by royal **charter**. This meant that the king of England gave the land and the right to settle it to a particular group or company. The king made the rules for government. New Hampshire, on the other hand, began as a **proprietary** colony. The king gave land in New Hampshire to a company of businessmen called the Council for New England. The council then gave large areas of land directly to particular people, who controlled the property like landlords. New Hampshire later became a royal colony under the direct control of the king.

natural resource—something useful or valuable; wood, for example is a natural resource that is used for building houses and furniture

charter—an official document granting permission to set up a new colony, organization, or company

proprietary—belonging to a property owner

Early Reports

In the 1500s and 1600s, explorers and fur traders from Europe sailed to America. They sent reports back to Europe telling of America's treasures. They described friendly natives and thick forests, large lakes, and wide rivers full of fish. In 1603 an Englishman named Martin Pring arrived on the New Hampshire coast with two small ships, the *Speedwell* and the *Discoverer*. With a crew of 43 men and two large dogs, he explored the lower Piscataqua River near present-day Portsmouth. He reported finding "Deere, Beares, Wolves, Foxes, Lusernes [lynxes] and Dogges with sharpe noses." He thought the area would be excellent for fur trading and fishing.

Europeans came to North America to trade.

NEW HAMPSHIRE

Champlain

French explorer Samuel de Champlain also explored the Atlantic coast. Unlike others, he traveled inland and discovered major rivers and lakes. Champlain visited New Hampshire's White Mountains. In 1609 he explored a lake that would be named for him. Lake Champlain is located on the present-day Vermont–New York border. Native American chiefs guided him on his journeys. Although he was among the first Europeans to explore New Hampshire, he did not encourage the French king to establish colonies there. He suggested the French develop colonies in Nova Scotia and Quebec to the north, in what is now Canada.

From Native Americans, traders bought animal furs in exchange for blankets, pots, and weapons. This is an artist's idea of what the trading might have looked like.

New England

In April 1614 Englishman John Smith sailed north from Virginia. He reported on his journeys and drew a map of the coast, which he named New England. Smith hoped to find gold and silver. Instead he found fish, fur, and trees tall enough to be used as **masts** for ships. John Smith sent his findings to England's King James I. The king, who saw the value in establishing colonies in America, set up a council for the "ruling and governing of New England in America." The king wanted the council to determine how New Hampshire would develop.

In New England John Smith found forests full of animals.

Critical Thinking with Primary Sources

John Smith mapped what he called New England in 1614. What types of features do you notice on Smith's map? Why do you think he included them? What was he trying to show?

"Here should be no landlords to rack [torture] us with high rents, or ... fines to consume us. Here every man may be master of his own labor and land in a short time."

—Captain John Smith writing about New Hampshire in 1614.

mast—a tall pole on a ship's deck that holds its sails

Chapter 1:
New Hampshire's Native People

Long before English settlers arrived, the Abenaki people lived in eastern New Hampshire and Maine. The Pennacooks lived in central and southern New Hampshire. Both tribes spoke the Algonquian language. In the coastal areas, New Hampshire colonists were most likely to meet Pennacook people.

Daily Life

The Pennacooks were farmers and hunters. They grew corn, beans, and squash. Women cared for the crops while the men hunted and fished. Native hunters used bows and arrows to kill moose, deer, bear, and other game. They often speared fish in summer or fished through the ice in winter.

Wigwams, which provided protection from the weather, were quick and easy to build.

The Pennacooks lived in wigwams. Wigwams were made of young trees bent to form low, round huts. They were covered with bark or animal skins. Villages were made up of wigwams built close together for protection. There were several Pennacook villages on the banks of the Merrimack River.

The Pennacooks built villages along New Hampshire's Merrimack River.

Effects of Disease

Prior to 1600 there were probably about 3,000 Pennacooks in the region. Thousands of Native Americans had already died from diseases, such as **smallpox** and measles, brought by European explorers and traders. The natives had no **resistance** to the diseases. By 1613 only about 300 Pennacooks remained.

smallpox—a disease that spreads easily from person to person, causing chills, fever, and pimples that scar
resistance—the ability to fight off a disease

This illustration is an artist's idea of native people trading furs.

Colonists and Natives

At first the colonists and the natives got along well. The English settlers traded goods like shirts, coats, and kettles for land. However, the Native Americans wanted to keep the lands they had cleared for farms. The first settlers agreed because they did not intend to become farmers.

The knowledge the colonists gained from the Native Americans helped them survive. The colonists learned to build canoes, hunt, fish, and plant as the Native Americans did. Furs bought from Native Americans kept colonists warm during the harsh winters. Native American medicines, developed from native plants, helped them stay healthy. For about 50 years, relationships between settlers and Native Americans were peaceful.

Passaconaway

Passaconaway was the sachem, or chief, of the Pennacooks when English settlers first arrived. Passaconaway's people believed that he had magical powers. Some claimed he could make water burn, rocks move, and trees dance. Under his leadership the Pennacook population increased and their territory expanded.

In 1644 Passaconaway met with English leaders and agreed to follow their authority. In 1662 Passaconaway asked the Colonial government to set aside land for his people. They agreed, but in 1729 the land was taken back and sold to colonists.

Did You Know?

According to historians Passaconaway gave a farewell speech to his people when he was over 100 years old. He told them that peace was the only hope for them.

Chapter 2:
Founding of New Hampshire

In 1621 the Council for New England gave a land **grant** to Captain John Mason. Mason named the land New Hampshire after his home county of Hampshire, England. Sir Ferdinando Gorges, who headed the Council for New England, also claimed a large area of land in present-day Maine. Gorges and Mason set up the Laconia Company, which lent money to colonists. The colonists would repay the company with money earned through fur trading and fishing.

In 1623 English colonists established a settlement called Pannaway in New Hampshire.

First Settlers

The Laconia Company sent David Thompson to New Hampshire to set up a colony. Thompson arrived in 1623 with about 10 men and their families. His settlement, Pannaway Plantation, was located in present-day Rye. The settlers built a large stone house surrounded by a high wall mounted with guns and cannons. Historians believe David Thompson's son, John, was the first English child born in New Hampshire. Thompson and his family did not remain long. Around 1627 they moved to Boston.

"The next place I came into was Pannaway, where one Mr. Thomson hath made a plantation. There I stayed about one month, the weather being very unseasonable and very much snow. In these parts I saw much good timber, but the ground it seemed to me not to be good, being very rocky and full of trees and brushwood."

—Captain Christopher Levett, a sea captain who visited Pannaway in 1623–24.

Did You Know?

Because New Hampshire has so much of the hard rock called granite, it is known as "The Granite State."

grant—a gift such as land or money given for a particular purpose

Dover

Brothers Edward and William Hilton had settled at Pannaway with David Thompson. The Hiltons set up a fishery and built **saltworks** in order to preserve the fish with salt. In 1623 the Hiltons established their own settlement, Northam, seven miles up the Cochecho River. Northam, now called Dover, became New Hampshire's first permanent settlement. When the Hiltons moved to Northam, they took several farmers from Pannaway with them. This group built houses, planted corn, and traded with local natives for furs and other goods.

Dover was New Hampshire's first permanent settlement.

Did You Know?

Dover is the seventh oldest town in the United States.

In 1640 Portsmouth was a small settlement called Strawbery Banke.

Strawbery Banke

In 1632 the Laconia Company sent another 66 men and 22 women from England. They brought equipment for fishing and logging, seeds for planting, and manufactured items to trade with the Native Americans. One member of the group, Walter Neale, set up a trading post on the Piscataqua River using Thompson's house at Pannaway.

Another settler, Thomas Warnerton, established a settlement called Strawbery Banke at present-day Portsmouth. It was named for the wild strawberries that grew there. Settlers built a large house called Mason Hall. A strong wall with eight cannons surrounded Mason Hall. Settlers slowly built more homes and planted gardens to provide food. Fishing, shipbuilding, and trade of various kinds helped Strawbery Banke grow and prosper.

saltworks—a building where salt is made

Four Towns

While most New Hampshire settlements were founded to make money, Exeter was founded for a different reason. John Wheelwright and a small group of religious followers had been ordered to leave Massachusetts. They had not obeyed religious leaders there. In 1638 Wheelwright bought land in New Hampshire and established the town of Exeter. Exeter became New Hampshire's fourth permanent settlement after Dover, Strawbery Banke, and Hampton, which was founded earlier in 1638.

Many settlers in New Hampshire were fishermen, farmers, or hunters. Fur trading was still big business, but logging was becoming more and more important. New Hampshire's tall pine trees were an excellent source of lumber. Loggers cut down the trees and prepared them for shipment to England, where they were sold as masts. New Hampshire's trees were also used in building homes, ships, and furniture.

John Wheelwright founded the town of Exeter.

Did You Know?

Exeter was the state of New Hampshire's first capital city.

Meanwhile, the fishing operation that began at Pannaway was moved to the Isles of Shoals just off the coast. The Isles of Shoals became the center of the colony's fishing industry.

During the 1600s and 1700s, New Hampshire's forests provided lumber for ship masts.

Massachusetts in Charge

By 1640 New Hampshire had a population of around 1,000 people. About half of New Hampshire's settlers were people who moved north from Massachusetts. But the settlers weren't governed as well as they were in Massachusetts. They lacked a single government. Eventually New Hampshire let the Massachusetts Bay Colony take charge. The four towns needed the protection and safety of a larger and more powerful colony. By 1641 Massachusetts gained control of New Hampshire's land and settlements.

Chapter 3:
Growing Colony

At first the colonists depended on England for livestock and supplies. They **imported** sheep, oxen, and chickens, as well as wheat and other foods. They also imported apple and pear trees to make cider and "perry," a kind of pear beer. Colonists soon discovered local fruits and berries like grapes, strawberries, and raspberries. The colonists also imported guns, ammunition, and fishing tackle from England.

Codfish were one of New Hampshire's major exports.

Trade

Early colonists had hoped to trade with the Pennacook and Abenaki people. They established trading posts along the coast of Maine and on the Merrimack River. But the market in Europe for these goods was not as strong as the colonists expected. So New Hampshire colonists began trading with Massachusetts. They sent cattle and hogs south in exchange for salt, sugar, flour, and wine imported from Europe and other colonies.

By the 1650s New Hampshire shipped fish, especially cod, to England for high profits. Lumber brought worldwide recognition to the colony. By 1700 there were 90 sawmills along New Hampshire's rivers. In 1671 New Hampshire merchants shipped 500 tons of fish and thousands of furs to Europe. They also **exported** more than 50 masts that year.

Colonists traded with natives for items such as furs and this Pennacook basket.

import—to bring goods into one country from another
export—to send and sell goods to other countries

A Growing Colony

By the late 1600s, New Hampshire's seacoast towns were well established. Several new towns had also developed, mostly along the rivers. Many people produced their own food through gardening, hunting, and fishing. If they had more than they needed, they traded for supplies at town markets. As time went on, many colonists purchased additional land so that their children could become farmers too. During the winter months, farmers often took jobs logging or working in sawmills.

Not everyone farmed. Some men worked as fishermen or shipbuilders. Others were craftsmen who made fine furniture or metal items. Every town also had merchants who had become wealthy from trade.

New Hampshire towns were well organized.

The Massachusetts government allowed the New Hampshire towns to govern themselves. Each town established its own laws and tried to keep taxes low. They held town meetings to elect officials. All male landowners could vote in these elections. The voters elected five or six **selectmen** to oversee the running of the town.

Many towns also elected a "fence viewer," who made sure fences were mended, and a sheriff to enforce the laws. Most young or able men joined the **militia**. The militia protected towns from Native American attacks.

Did You Know?

New Hampshire has the shortest coastline of any state in the United States that borders an ocean.

New Hampshire's tall trees were good for shipbuilding.

selectman—a government official in a New England town

militia—a group of volunteer citizens who are organized to fight but are not professional soldiers

Daily Life

Early New Hampshire colonists lived in one-room wooden houses. As families grew they added more rooms. A fireplace was used for cooking. It provided heat and light too. Even so, Colonial houses were cold in winter as wind seeped through cracks between the boards. To preserve heat, houses had small windows. At night people used candles or oil lamps for light.

Girls helped their mothers care for younger children, prepare meals, knit, and work in the garden. Sons learned their fathers' trades. For example, sons of farmers cleared the land, built fences, and cared for animals. Sons of shipbuilders learned to build ships.

Fireplaces kept Colonial homes warm.

The artist's illustration shows what might have happened in a Colonial schoolroom. A student may have been made to wear a dunce cap for misbehaving.

A 1693 law required towns to provide schools. But even if a town built a school, there was a shortage of teachers. Educated men taught their sons to read and sent them to Harvard College in Massachusetts for further education. Some girls learned to read from their mothers or at school, but girls were not allowed to go to college.

Chapter 4:
Royal Colony

For several years New Hampshire towns managed their own affairs with little interference from Massachusetts. However, in 1650 the relatives of John Mason, the original landowner, wanted to **reclaim** his land. The debate in England about who owned New Hampshire brought about many changes. The most important occurred in 1679, when the British government made New Hampshire a royal colony with a governor of its own. Massachusetts was no longer in charge.

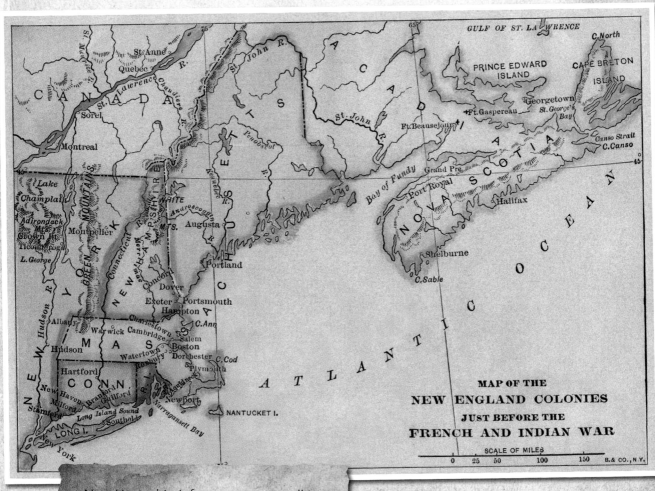

MAP OF THE
NEW ENGLAND COLONIES
JUST BEFORE THE
FRENCH AND INDIAN WAR

New Hampshire's four towns were all in the southeastern part of the colony, close to the colony of Massachusetts.

This 19th century illustration shows Governor Andros taken prisoner in Boston.

Seven years later England's King James II made more changes by creating the Dominion of New England. The Dominion put the Northern Colonies under one government structure. In 1686 the king sent Sir Edward Andros to Boston to take control of Massachusetts and New Hampshire. Soon Rhode Island and Connecticut were added to the Dominion of New England. New York and New Jersey joined in 1688. Under this government, laws were strict and taxes were high.

A rebellion in England led to the defeat of James II in 1688. On April 18, 1689, New England also rebelled and arrested Andros. England's new rulers, King William and Queen Mary, restored the former Colonial governments. That meant Massachusetts controlled New Hampshire again. But the new king worried about Massachusetts becoming too powerful. He sent his own governor to take control of New Hampshire. Finally, in 1692, New Hampshire again became a royal colony.

reclaim—to take or claim again

King William's War

Although relations with the native people had been mostly good, problems increased when France and England began fighting in Europe. When the fighting carried over to America, the French **enlisted** some native tribes to fight the English. England enlisted other tribes to fight the French. King William's War (1689–1697) was the first of several wars in America between the French and English. The first attack on New Hampshire came in 1689, when Native Americans attacked Dover. They killed 23 settlers and captured 29 others. From 1689 until the end of the French and Indian War in 1763, New Hampshire colonists lived in constant fear of Native American attacks.

An artist's depiction shows the surprise attack on Dover.

Hannah Dustin (1657–1736?)

On March 15, 1697, Native Americans attacked the village of Haverhill, Massachusetts. Thomas Dustin led his children to safety. His wife, Hannah, who had just given birth, was unable to escape. Hannah, the baby, and her nurse were taken captive. The baby died, but Hannah and the nurse traveled over 150 miles north. One night, while the Native Americans slept, Hannah killed her captors and escaped. She became the first woman in America to be honored with a statue. It still stands at Boscawen, New Hampshire.

Hannah Dustin's escape made her a heroine.

"I am Thankful for my Captivity, 'twas the Comfortablest [meaning the most spiritually and morally strengthening] time that ever I had; In my Affliction God made his Word Comfortable to me."

—Hannah Dustin, 1724

enlist—to voluntarily join a branch of the military

Protecting Towns

After King William's War ended in 1697, the French and English fought a series of other wars known as the French and Indian wars. The two nations battled over control of land in North America. Colonists and native people were caught in the middle, and New Hampshire towns were often the first attacked. As a result, few new towns were founded, and older towns used their resources to build **garrisons** for protection. Growth slowed. Many New Hampshire men left their farms to go to war, so crops suffered. The war even affected fishing. Fishermen working along the coast feared attack from French ships. A treaty signed in Paris in 1763 would give England most of France's land in North America. Peace finally returned to the New Hampshire frontier.

New Hampshire volunteers helped the British take the French Fortress of Louisbourg in Canada. This event would lead them to winning the war and gaining peace.

The Fort at No. 4 protected settlements along the Connecticut River.

The Fort at No. 4

By the mid-1700s, the fighting had shifted to the west, along the Connecticut River. In the 1740s Massachusetts set up four forts to defend against enemy attack. The Fort at No. 4, located at present-day Charlestown, New Hampshire, was attacked most often. For nearly 20 years it remained the northernmost English settlement in New Hampshire. Despite frequent attacks, the fort was never destroyed. Later it became an important gathering point during the Revolutionary War.

garrison—a fort or other structure built for protection

New Towns, New Settlers

Progress and growth resumed again. In 1719 Scots-Irish people from northern Ireland began to settle the town of Londonderry and successfully grew Irish potatoes. Soon potatoes became popular throughout the colonies. Other settlers were attracted to New Hampshire's shipbuilding industry. It brought in workers from British shipyards. Seacoast towns expanded, but development was slower on the frontier. Upper Ashuelot, present-day Keene, was settled in 1736.

Critical Thinking with Primary Sources

The Queen of Sheba Admiring the Wisdom of Solomon needlepoint was created by Mary Williams of New Hampshire in 1744. It shows a story from the Bible, but the homes and people are shown in Colonial style. What can you learn about Colonial life from what is shown here? What do you notice about the way the people are dressed?

Royal Governor

In 1741 Benning Wentworth became governor of New Hampshire. As governor he could charter towns, select judges, and control elections. Wentworth created 129 new townships. He made Portsmouth the colony's capital and encouraged population growth and trade.

In 1744 Wentworth joined the governor of Massachusetts in supporting a surprise attack on the French Fortress at Louisbourg, Nova Scotia. Capturing the Fortress at Louisbourg in 1745 helped England win the French and Indian War. It also increased Wentworth's popularity. Even so, colonists claimed that Wentworth had grown rich by setting aside land for himself. When he was forced to retire in 1767, his nephew John took over.

Benning Wentworth (1696–1770)

Born in Portsmouth, New Hampshire, Benning Wentworth came from a wealthy business family. Wentworth graduated from Harvard in 1715 and joined the family business as a merchant. In 1741, when he was 44, Wentworth became New Hampshire's first royal governor. When he retired in 1767, he was one of the richest men in New England.

Did You Know?

It is believed that the first white potato planted in America was in Derry, New Hampshire, in 1719.

Chapter 5:
Revolt!

The British government needed money to pay for the French and Indian War. They decided to tax the colonists. In 1764 the British government approved the Sugar Act, which required colonists to pay a tax on molasses. In 1765 the Quartering Act required colonists to provide housing for British troops. That same year, the Stamp Act taxed paper items such as legal documents, playing cards, and newspapers. In Portsmouth citizens forced the tax collector to resign. Protests throughout the colonies forced the British government to **repeal** the Stamp Act in 1766 before any taxes were collected.

On September 12, 1765, Portsmouth citizens hung an effigy, or a crude model, of a stamp agent to protest the Stamp Act.

John Wentworth

When John Wentworth became governor in 1767, the population of New Hampshire had reached 52,000 people. Portsmouth, the biggest city, had 4,500 residents. Wentworth began governing by inspecting the forests. His travels led him to propose a road system to ease communication between distant settlements. He divided the colony into five counties, each with its own court. He encouraged trade and improved the colony's finances.

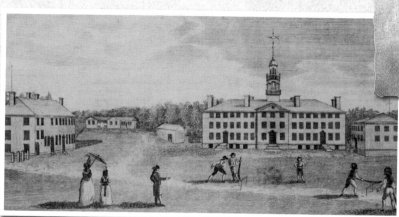

Dartmouth College was founded in 1769 on land granted by John Wentworth.

In 1769 Wentworth granted land to establish Dartmouth College in Hanover. Dartmouth is America's ninth oldest college. It was founded "for the education and instruction of Youth of the Indian Tribes in this Land ... and also of English Youth and any others."

"... I soon determined that the grand secret of peace ... was to cause them to think before they acted ..."
—John Wentworth, 1767

Did You Know?

Dartmouth's first graduating class in 1771 had only four students.

The Pine Tree Riot

While New Hampshire developed, Britain had made laws the New Englanders did not like. One such law said that white pine trees had to be saved for shipbuilding by the British Navy. Because of the law, colonists had to pay fees to cut down white pines on their land. Many New Hampshire colonists refused to obey the law. However, Governor Wentworth insisted on enforcing the law. In one notable instance, a sheriff was sent to arrest a mill owner who did not obey the law. A protest by many colonists became violent. The sheriff was forced to leave to get help to control them. But when he returned, the protesters were gone. The event became known as the Pine Tree Riot of 1772.

The Governor's Mistake

Most New Hampshire colonists were farmers or laborers. They opposed British taxes and other restrictions on their freedom. So did the New Hampshire Assembly, which was made up of representatives from the various towns. In October 1774 Royal Governor Wentworth sent several carpenters to Boston to help build lodging for British soldiers. The colonists were furious! It wasn't long before they joined other colonies in a rebellion against Britain.

John Langdon (1741–1819)

Born near Portsmouth, John Langdon was a wealthy merchant before entering politics. He helped lead New Hampshire throughout the Revolutionary War as speaker of the New Hampshire House. He devoted his time to reorganizing the New Hampshire militia and spent his own money to pay for their equipment. In 1785 he became governor of New Hampshire. He also helped write the U.S. Constitution. From 1789 to 1801, he served as a U.S. senator. He died in Portsmouth in 1819.

Paul Revere's First Ride

On December 13, 1774, Paul Revere left Boston for Portsmouth, New Hampshire. He brought news that the British planned to take the arms from Fort William and Mary in New Castle, New Hampshire, before the Patriots could get it. The following day, John Langdon, a devoted Patriot, led 400 other New Hampshire Patriots to the fort. Royal Governor Wentworth tried to stop them, but they carried away 100 barrels of gunpowder and locked up the fort's guards. When the news of the Patriots' success reached other rebels, more volunteers went back to the fort. They removed the remaining cannons and other weapons before the British arrived. Wentworth tried to recruit more soldiers to defend the fort, but no one helped him. Too many people were already part of the uprising. They distributed the stolen weapons and ammunition to Patriots throughout the region.

War

In January 1775 New Hampshire representatives met in Exeter to discuss independence. They warned colonists to prepare for war. On April 19, 1775, the Revolutionary War officially began with battles in Lexington and Concord, Massachusetts. In June around 5,000 British soldiers were stationed in the Boston area. Nearly 1,200 New Hampshire militiamen marched to Boston to help fight the British.

A few days later, about 2,500 American troops secured Breed's Hill against the British. They mistook it for Bunker Hill. Though the Americans were defeated, they lost fewer soldiers than the British. At least 107 New Hampshire soldiers died during the Battle of Bunker Hill. However, the battle gave the Americans confidence that they could fight the British Army.

NEW HAMPSHIRE

The New Hampshire militia fought in the Battle of Bunker Hill.

New Hampshire forces defeated the British at the Battle of Bennington.

Although no battles were fought on New Hampshire soil, about 18,500 New Hampshire men fought in the Revolutionary War. New Hampshire military leaders such as John Stark, John Sullivan, Enoch Poor, and James Reed helped America to victory. At the Battle of Bennington in August 1777, Stark met the British near the Vermont–New York border. He led 1,500 New Hampshire men and a small force from Vermont to stop the British from restocking their supplies. Stark's men killed over 200 British soldiers and took another 700 prisoner. Stark reported that 30 Americans died.

John Stark (1728–1822)

John Stark earned fame for his bravery during the French and Indian War (1754–1763). He also fought at Bunker Hill. In 1775 he was made a colonel in the 1st New Hampshire Regiment. He became a general in 1777, just before his success at the Battle of Bennington. In other battles he helped force the British to surrender. He retired from the army in 1783 and lived on his farm until his death in 1822.

New Hampshire Becomes a State

A few New Hampshire merchants remained loyal to England. However, most New Hampshire colonists favored independence. William Whipple, Matthew Thornton, and Josiah Bartlett represented New Hampshire in signing the Declaration of Independence. New Hampshire was the first of the 13 Colonies to set up its own government. In January 1776 New Hampshire representatives drafted a constitution. On September 11, 1776, the colony created its own state government.

A New Government

The new state government of New Hampshire was busy. It established a court system and a financial system, wrote several new laws, and tried to establish a western border. About 100 towns that had formed under Governor Benning Wentworth were located west of the Connecticut River. In July 1777 these towns declared their independence as the state of Vermont. For a while, 36 towns on the eastern side of the river joined them. Eventually the Connecticut River became the dividing line between New Hampshire and Vermont.

The state seal shows a part of New Hampshire's Colonial history. The warship *Raleigh* in its center was part of the new Continental navy. It was built in Portsmouth in 1776 and may have carried the first American flag into sea battle.

During the war the Continental Congress wrote articles that set up the country's first national government. In September 1787 representatives met in Philadelphia to sign the U.S. Constitution. New Hampshire's representatives took their time considering the new nation's Constitution. On June 21, 1788, it **ratified** the U.S. Constitution, making New Hampshire the ninth state to join the United States.

Critical Thinking with Primary Sources

Joseph Frederick Wallet Des Barres sketched this view of Portsmouth in 1780. What do you notice on the Piscataqua River? Take a closer look at the city across the river. What kinds of buildings do you see?

ratify—to formally approve

Timeline

1602 Bartholomew Gosnold explores the coast of New England for English merchants.

1603 Martin Pring goes ashore in New Hampshire.

1614 Captain John Smith maps the New England coastline.

1620 King James I establishes the Council for New England.

1622 The Council for New England grants land to John Mason and Sir Ferdinando Gorges.

1623 David Thompson establishes the Pannaway Plantation at Rye. The Hilton brothers found the town of Northam, later renamed Dover.

1629 John Mason names New Hampshire.

1638 Exeter and Hampton are founded.

1641 Massachusetts claims control over New Hampshire.

1650 John Mason's family takes Massachusetts to court over land rights.

1679 New Hampshire becomes a royal colony.

1690 Massachusetts takes back control of New Hampshire.

1692 New Hampshire is made a royal colony for the second time.

1719 The first potatoes in the American Colonies are planted at Derry, New Hampshire.

1741 Benning Wentworth becomes governor of New Hampshire.

1767 John Wentworth becomes governor of New Hampshire.

1769 Dartmouth College is founded at Hanover.

1774 New Hampshire colonists seize control of Fort William and Mary from the British and hide gunpowder and weapons stored there.

1775 The Revolutionary War begins in April. In June, the New Hampshire militia fights at the Battle of Bunker Hill under John Stark.

1776 The 13 Colonies formally declare their independence in July. In September the New Hampshire House of Representatives forms a state government.

1777 In July the towns west of the Connecticut River form the state of Vermont. The Battle of Bennington takes place in August.

1783 The Revolutionary War ends with the signing of the Treaty of Paris. Great Britain officially recognizes the United States as an independent nation.

1788 New Hampshire becomes the ninth state of the United States when it ratifies the U.S. Constitution.

"Live free or die."

—John Stark wrote these words in 1809 when he was invited to an anniversary celebration of the Battle of Bennington. It became New Hampshire's state motto in 1945.

Glossary

charter (CHAR-tuhr)—an official document granting permission to set up a new colony, organization, or company

colony (KAH-luh-nee)—a place that is settled by people from another country and is controlled by that country

enlist (in-LIST)—to voluntarily join a branch of the military

export (EK-sport)—to send and sell goods to other countries

garrison (GA-ruh-suhn)—a fort or other structure built for protection

grant (GRANT)—a gift such as land or money given for a particular purpose

import (IM-port)—to bring goods into one country from another

mast (MAST)—a tall pole on a ship's deck that holds its sails

militia (muh-LISH-uh)—a group of volunteer citizens who are organized to fight but are not professional soldiers

natural resource (NACH-ur-uhl REE-sorss)—something useful or valuable; wood, for example, is a natural resource that is useful for building houses and furniture

proprietary (proh-PREYE-uh-ter-ee)—belonging to a property owner

ratify (RAT-uh-fye)—to formally approve

reclaim (ri-KLAYM)—to take or claim again

repeal (ri-PEEL)—to officially cancel something, such as a law

resistance (ri-ZISS-tuhnss)—the ability to fight off a disease

saltworks (SAWLT-wurks)—a building where salt is made

selectman (si-LEKT-muhn)—a government official in a New England town

smallpox (SMAWL-poks)—a disease that spreads easily from person to person, causing chills, fever, and pimples that scar

Critical Thinking Using the Common Core

1. How did New Hampshire get its name? (Key Ideas and Details)
2. What can you learn from the primary source features that you cannot find in the text? Why do you think these features were included? (Craft and Structure)
3. Which events might have added to the unhappiness of the colonists, leading them to fight a war for their independence? (Integration of Knowledge and Ideas)

Read More

Cunningham, Kevin. *The New Hampshire Colony*. New York: Children's Press, 2012.

Micklos, John Jr. *The Making of the United States from Thirteen Colonies through Primary Sources*. Berkeley Heights, N.J.: Enslow Publishers, 2013.

Pratt, Mary K. *A Timeline History of the Thirteen Colonies*. Minneapolis, Minn.: Lerner Publications, 2014.

Yale, Dallas. *The Colony of New Hampshire*. New York: PowerKids Press, 2016.

Internet Sites

FactHound offers a safe, fun way to find Internet sites related to this book. All of the sites on FactHound have been researched by our staff.
Here's all you do:
Visit *www.facthound.com*
Type in this code: 9781515722366

 **Super-cool stuff!** Check out projects, games and lots more at **www.capstonekids.com**

Source Notes

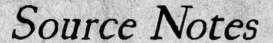

Page 6, line 15 quote: Martin Pring. "The Voyage of Martin Pring, 1603." *Early English and French Voyages: Chiefly from Hakluyt, 1534–1608*. Edited by Henry S. Burrage. New York: Charles Scribner's Sons, 1906, p. 346.

Page 8, lines 7–8: Elizabeth Forbes and Elting E. Morison. *New Hampshire: A Bicentennial History*, New York: W. W. Norton, 1976, p. 9.

Page 9, callout quote: "A Brief History of New Hampshire." NH.gov. 2011. Accessed April 13, 2016. http://www.nh.gov/nhinfo/history.html.

Page 15, callout quote: Langdon Brown Parsons. *History of the Town of Rye, New Hampshire, from Its Discovery and Settlement to December 31, 1903.* Concord, N.H.: Rumford Printing Company, 1905, p. 13.

Page 29, callout quote: Hannah Dustin. "Hannah Dustin's Letter to the Elders of the Second Church in Haverhill, 1724. (Haverhill Historical Society)." HawthorneinSalem.org. Accessed April 13, 2016. http://www.hawthorneinsalem.org/page/11866/

Page 35, line 11: "About the Native American Program." *Dartmouth University Native American Program*. Accessed April 13, 2016. https://www.dartmouth.edu/~nap/about/.

Page 35, callout quote: *John Wentworth, Governor of New Hampshire, 1767–1775*, by Lawrence Shaw Mayo. Cambridge, Mass.: Harvard University Press, 1921, p. 122.

Page 43, callout quote: "State Emblem" NH.gov. Accessed April 13, 2016. https://www.nh.gov/nhinfo/emblem.html.

Regions of the 13 Colonies		
Northern Colonies	**Middle Colonies**	**Southern Colonies**
Connecticut, Massachusetts, New Hampshire, Rhode Island	Delaware, New Jersey, New York, Pennsylvania	Georgia, Maryland, North Carolina, South Carolina, Virginia
land more suitable for hunting than farming; trees cut down for lumber; trapped wild animals for their meat and fur; fished in rivers, lakes, and ocean	the "Breadbasket" colonies—rich farmland, perfect for growing wheat, corn, rye, and other grains	soil better for growing tobacco, rice, and indigo; crops grown on huge farms called plantations; landowners depended heavily on servants and slaves to work in the fields

Select Bibliography

Bahmueller, Charles F., ed. The 50 States. Pasadena, Calif.: Salem Press, 2007.

Barker, Shirley. Builders of New England. New York: Dodd, Mead & Company, 1965.

Daniell, Jere R. Colonial New Hampshire: A History. Millwood, N.Y.: KTO Press, 1981.

Dustin, Hannah. "Hannah Dustin's Letter to the Elders of the Second Church in Haverhill, 1724. (Haverhill Historical Society)." HawthorneinSalem.org. Accessed April 13, 2016. http://www.hawthorneinsalem.org/page/11866/.

Faragher, John Mack. The Encyclopedia of Colonial and Revolutionary America. New York: Facts on File, 1990.

Fry, William Henry. New Hampshire as a Royal Province. New York: AMS, 1908.

Gale Cenage Learning. Explorers & Discoverers of the World. Gale Biography In Context, 1993.

Hill, Ralph Nading. Yankee Kingdom: Vermont and New Hampshire. New York: Harper & Row, 1960.

Leach, Douglas Edward. The Northern Colonial Frontier 1607–1763. New York: Holt, Rinehart and Winston, 1966.

Magill, Frank N. and John L. Loos, eds. Great Events from History: 15,000 B.C. – 1819, rev. ed. Vol. 1, North American Series. Pasadena, Calif.: Salem Press, 1997.

Malinowski, Sharon and Anna Sheets, eds. The Gale Encyclopedia of Native American Tribes. Vol. 1, Northeast, Southeast, Caribbean. Detroit: Gale, 1998.

Mayo, Lawrence Shaw. John Wentworth, Governor of New Hampshire, 1767–1775. Cambridge, Mass.: Harvard University Press, 1921.

Middleton, Richard. Colonial America: A History, 1565–1776. Malden, Mass.: Blackwell, 2002.

Morison, Elizabeth Forbes and Elting E. Morison. New Hampshire: A Bicentennial History, New York: W. W. Norton, 1976.

"New Hampshire Almanac." NH.gov. Accessed January 19, 2016. https://www.nh.gov/nhinfo/index.html.

Parsons, Langdon Brown. History of the Town of Rye, New Hampshire, from Its Discovery and Settlement to December 31, 1903. Concord, N.H.: Rumford Printing Company, 1905.

Pring, Martin. "The Voyage of Martin Pring, 1603." Early English and French Voyages: Chiefly from Hakluyt, 1534–1608. Edited by Henry S. Burrage. New York: Charles Scribner's Sons, 1906. 345–52.

Purvis, Thomas L. Colonial America to 1763. Almanacs of American Life. New York: Facts on File, 1999.

Smith, John. A Description of New England, or the Observations and Discoveries of Captain John Smith. Rochester, N.Y.: George P. Humphrey, 1898.

Index